When We Feel We Exist

When We Feel We Exist

Other Projects by Dre Hill

i love you means nothing

Melanin "Black"

Crossroads

(No) I am (not) okay

Pushing the Pen: A Poetry Prompt Book

existence is more than puffs of air
rushing in and out of lungs in a
metaphorical haste for living—
each and every sensory moment
makes the taps and tingles from
fingertips mean something.
it is in these moments that we matter.
when we feel, that is when we exist.

It's more than just words on a page. Scan the QR code below to access the When We Feel, We Exist playlist on Spotify. Listen and enjoy!

Table of Contents

plastic, propaganda, and the cycle of recycling   15
Bloody Gingiva   16
Heavy   17
A Note on Pain   18
Hunger Pains   19
Mondays   20
Waiting   21
chilled   22
Tranquil   23
After the 5   24
morning's rays   25
The Weekend   26
Lemonade   27
Sex on the Beach   28
Bubbles   29
in this season I choose joy   30
Smile   31
puppy love   32
Magic   33
I love the sunshine (Vitamin D)   34
Laughter   35
godwinks   36

plastic, propaganda, and the cycle of recycling

In a world full of authenticity
I am plastic
think of me like a game of charades
I am the master of playing pretend
after all, that's what it means, right?
to fake it until you make it

so, in a world full of authenticity
call me propaganda
I am recycled materials made new
like the same talking points regurgitated—
just clothed in a shiny, alluring new skin
regifted falsities from decades before

Bloody Gingiva

this is my ritual
spill my blood
watch it pool
it will feed the children
the forests will not thirst
I watch it melt into the soil
wash away in the rain
it spirals down the drain
I rinse my mouth
stopping when the bleeding does

Heavy

this is unlike eyelids
drooping with fatigue
lulled by the whispers
of a promised rest—
instead, this is lead
buried deep in one's chest
as if putting one to death,
goodbye and *goodnight*—
all a secret code that
calls you out of nightmares,
gasping—*grieving.*
in those shallow exhales
you gift the heaviness of
our world back to the atmosphere,
just to do it all over again.

A Note on Pain

pain is experiencing the inevitable
knowing that you are destined for disaster.
like a head-on collision
frozen like a deer in headlights—
awaiting impact.

sights
sounds
bones crushing immediately.
squelching noises
pain radiating everywhere,
it all being over in an instant.
then the deafening silence
after the cacophony—
stillness

Hunger Pains

pangs reverberate in echoes
like clock strikes chiming
this telltale sign
a tale as old as time
biological ordinance
governing when one should eat—
but there's solace in those pains
in signals coming from the brain
when chemistry and wiring work the same
all these subdermal sensations
ringing in symphony, singing—

let us eat.

Mondays
and every day that feels like it

dreary, dreadful
dark cloud overhead
precipitating slow drip
prescription doses of angst—
no one really waits for Monday
no one hopes Monday comes
knocking on their front door.
dread it
run from it
Monday comes all the same,
sucking the life out of the weekend party.
but, ponder this question—
is not this cycle of dreaded
decline the truest sign of life?
continue to hate your Mondays,
along with every day
that feels like it.
it's just another way of
saying you're alive

Waiting

minutes
stretching
dripping into hours
circling the drain

hours
extending
unfolding into days
unfurling like limbs

days
running
gliding into weeks
fading like daylight

weeks
blending
morphing into months
falling into years

waiting
watching
listening to signs
acting on faith

chilled

frost-riddled tongues
lay waste to bare cheeks
raw with irritation—
burning hot with red
like blushing, flushed,
all while we blow kisses
or send snowstorms into
early morning skies.
these cold breaths are
battle cries or roars
from icy dragons.
sensations burst,
crackling like the
shattering of glaciers—
or the chill of mint
flavoring nipping
at the tastebuds.

Tranquil

stillness
shadows blanket
earthy grass beds
blinking in and out
of windows carved
by rays of sunlight
through dewy, soft
windows made of clouds.
this stillness
I lay here
tucked in, swaddled
for a midday's nap
breathing in rhythm
as the wind dances
traipsing softly around
sleepy bodies.
loving this stillness

After the 5

voracious joy that
vibrates inside the body
stemming from the simple
act of shutting down—
shuttering brick and mortar,
saving files for later.
saying goodbye to storefront,
classroom, office, cubicle or
whatever confines that constitute
as your salary acquisition center—
flowery, fanciful words for a job
that you leave behind blissfully,
even on the greatest of days.
keys in hand, ready to unwind

morning's rays

early mornings glow
with ethereal nectar,
blowing golden lava
across the sky.
light speckles like
spillover splashing
against every surface—
skin soaks it in
as flesh mounds
fold and move, made
ceremonious with the
posture of breathwork
or prayer—soaking
up the silence from the
syllables spelt in the
atmosphere, as the earth
begins to stir and
morning's rays begin to
gently kiss us awake.

The Weekend
<that Friday feeling>

I sip on slow drip breaths
often held subconsciously—
trapping afterimages and
faint echoes from weeks before

I swallow these remnant residuals
in the biting of my tongue—
tamping down on slow-cooked
curses for early morning alarms

I spit out the taste acquired
from hours of repetition—
marinating in the vestiges of
manufactured tasks for trade

I sigh

breathing in these two days of relief

Lemonade

Tart
Divine
Nectar
The days prolong
The temperatures rise
And the pitcher runs empty
Sweet
Yellow
Lagoon
As summer sweeps the land
It is pretty common to find
Lemonade in one's hand

Sex on the Beach

I take a deep breath
The sun beams down on me
Without hesitation
I dive in
The waves sparkle
Diamonds in liquid motion
It is both cool
And warm
At the same time
This is sex on the beach
Sliding through the surf
Gritting sand in your teeth
Bursting through the surface
Lungs burning
As you pull a straw
From your empty
Mai Tai glass

Bubbles
[mimosa]

how refreshing,
bubbles suspended
holding space and time
floating on sweet rivers
that taste of nectar
much like the rapids
pulsating in my veins
though only one brings
both sweet relief and fantasy—
wrapped in the visage of
early morning sunrise,
as I dribble down the
side of my glass

apple
    orange
        peach
            pineapple

in this season I choose joy

I learned—
or rather, I recently realized
something about the secret to true joy
you see, joy is a verb
an action, an activity
somber words strung together,
slowly conjuring a smile
that's why they say
joy is an act of resistance
because of how you grapple
locked into a feral cage match
mirroring fists to face against reality
I understand now
why others say they choose joy
laying down their weapons of anguish
to carry something much lighter—
holding space for air, shining light like fire
in this season—I finally understand
as it oozes from my pores and
drips from the corners of my eyes
I, too, choose joy

Smile

A smile is the answer when
soft words fall on hardened ears,
like unstoppable forces
meeting immovable objects—*impasse.*
blocking out beautiful melodies
stretched out in decadence and
clicking like cadence, metronome.
hearing turned down as if
screaming into carpet flooring—
all things said lost to the void.
this ethereal sugar, serotonin nectar
shrunken down and carbonated
whilst sliding between luscious
portals and pearly gates.
settling the nerves and warming
everything like a cup of tea
on a cool winter's day.
soul shine, blinding,
beaming, effortlessly

puppy love

this love feels like adrenaline,
balls bouncing around walls
or the excitement of playing
tug-of-war with my favorite knot—
I palm you with passionate paws,
playing patty cake with your face.
each day is an opportunity in which
I shower you in kisses, nose to snout,
tongue to lips and cheek.
this love is forever—like the time between
belly rubs and sneaking treats.
all this, an illustration of the love
shared between human and their best friend.

Magic

I found magic in the way
you ride in on the wind—
effervescent movements caught in phases.
akin to lunar calendars or afterimages
caught chasing each burst in the
milliseconds between the shutter
and the flashing from the camera.
magic made into a moment—
moment into memory.
pausing like held breaths
stuttering silence counting
one hundred, two, until
everything comes into focus.
each memory strung together like
patchwork, life and relation
being the needle and thread.
home, strung together through
a series of photographs in sequence.

I love the sunshine (Vitamin D)

sunshine on me
filled with nectar
call it vitamin d
ghastly spectre
sunshine on me

bright projector
now you can see
mood protector
I'm finally free
my resurrector

sunshine on me
warm reception
sadness can flee
new perception
sunshine on me

I love the sunshine
sunshine on me
gotta love the sunshine
sunshine on me
sunshine on me

Laughter

unbridled joy begins
with deep-seated guffaws,
searching the throat canal
seeking a means of escape—
or maybe it's a squeal,
some kind of pitchy shriek,
scaring all whom are left
on the outside of the joke.
this unbridled joy leads to
laying on of hands, like
committing the body to God.
this joy runs like rivers
with bodies in flights,
limbs flowing every which way.
this, this is unbridled joy.

unbridled joy {laughs}

godwinks

quiet moments are deafening
indomitable silence stifled
by the voices of angels—
whispering in tones that
shrill like bells, wrapping
around the body like warm hugs.
in these moments—sun breaches,
breaking through the cloud cover,
creating small pockets shining
like glittery, golden hope.
all these, tiny echoes from earth,
as divine signs and wonders.

reassured—in these moments
      I clutch my heart
          tilt my head
               resting in the sky's lap

                    smiling

Acknowledgements

Writing a book, of any length or genre, is a communal labor of love. As the author, the burden to pour out soul onto the page, is shouldered alone. However, the support of community transmutes the scratches of script into the stitching and binding you hold in your hands. Or, the digital equivalent when swiping on your e-reader.

As always, I must start by thanking my family for constantly supporting me. You guys always show up for every event imaginable. You always promote me to your friends, classmates, and coworkers. Thank you, Mom, Dad, Alex, Shawn, Gaga, Jet, and the rest of the crew.

To my friends, you give me life always. Thank you for the late-night vents. For allowing me to send you incoherent snippets and musings. For showing up and supporting. Just like with my family, there is no universe in which I can do this without you. Thank you for keeping me grounded, level, and present in life so that I may pen every experience.

To my colleagues. Let's face it, y'all my friends too. Thank you for supporting me, loving on me, and creating space and opportunity for me when and where you can. Tati, Ayla, Olivia, Jasmine, Melissa, and everyone else! This would be like 10 pages if I could put all your names down and thank you individually. Just know I love you immensely and cherish your friendship, insight, and advice tremendously.

To my collaborators, Riel and Jocelyn, thank you for working with me patiently. In the midst of abstract thought, loose deadlines, and constant email threads you helped me make magic. I can't wait for our next adventure working together. Thank you immensely.

Lastly, thank you, dear reader. Thank you for giving my words and voice a shot. For inviting me into your safe space. Thank you for returning back, time and again. Without you, all of this would be for nothing. I hope this collection makes you feel something.

Meet the Author

Dre Hill is an artist, storyteller, educator, and apple juice enthusiast from Fort Worth, Tx where he currently resides. In 2021 he earned his B.A. in Animation and Writing, reigniting his passion for the written word. He is the author of multiple books including Melanin: Black, Crossroads, and the Indiverse Award winning (No) I am (not) okay. You can find Dre online @drehillart across various platforms. His website is drehillart.com.

www.ingramcontent.com/pod-product-compliance
Lightning Source LLC
Chambersburg PA
CBHW060258150626
46556CB00022B/3186